Count Your Way through
Africa

by Jim Haskins

illustrations by Barbara Knutson

Carolrhoda Books, Inc./Minneapolis

To Michael and Marcus

This book is available in two editions:
Library binding by Carolrhoda Books, Inc.,
 a division of Lerner Publishing Group
Soft cover by First Avenue Editions,
 an imprint of Lerner Publishing Group
241 First Avenue North
Minneapolis, MN 55401 U.S.A.

Website address: www.lernerbooks.com

Library of Congress Cataloging-in-Publication Data

Haskins, James, 1941–
  Count your way through Africa / by Jim Haskins ; illustrations by
Barbara Knutson.
     p.   cm.
  Summary: Uses the Swahili words for the numbers from one to ten
to introduce the land, history, and culture of Africa.
  ISBN 0-87614-347-8 (lib. bdg. : alk. paper)
  ISBN 0-87614-514-4 (pbk. : alk. paper)
  1. Africa—Civilization—Juvenile literature. 2. Counting—
Juvenile literature. [1. Africa. 2. Swahili language.
3. Counting.] I. Knutson, Barbara, ill. II. Title.
DT14.H36   1989
960—dc19   88-25896

Manufactured in the United States of America
15 16 17 18 19 20 – JR – 07 06 05 04 03 02

Introductory Note

The native peoples of Africa speak over 800 different languages, but we will count our way through Africa in Swahili. Swahili, also called Kiswahili, is a language widely spoken south of the Sahara Desert. It is the official language of Kenya and Tanzania. It is also used in other countries for business and for communication among people who speak different languages. In the modern, bustling cities of Africa, Swahili is often heard.

As early as the tenth century, and perhaps even before that, Swahili was used as a trading language. The Arabs, Persians, and East Indians who wished to trade with the tribal peoples on the eastern coast of Africa needed to be able to talk to them. So Swahili, which belongs to the group of languages called Bantu, gradually developed. Over the years, many Arabic, Persian, Hindi, Portuguese, and English words became part of the language.

Swahili uses the same alphabet as English. Although the consonants and vowels are sometimes combined differently than they would be in English, they are often pronounced the same, as you will see.

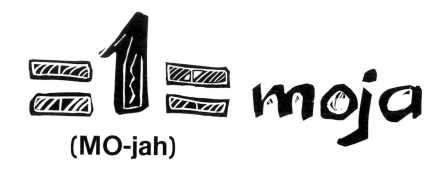

=1= moja

(MO-jah)

Africa is **one** continent, the second largest in the world. It is a continent of great variety, including two different climates. When winter comes to the south, summer begins in the north.

On this one continent are many different nations and peoples, religions and customs. The huge Sahara Desert divides the continent into northern and southern Africa. Most of the people who live in northern Africa are Arabian. In southern Africa, there are many different cultures and languages.

mbili

(mm-BEE-lee)

Ivory from the **two** tusks of the African elephant was an important product for traders in the 1500s. Africa was also rich in gold and other valuables. People from Western countries came to Africa to collect these treasures to sell in their homelands.

But not all traders came to find gold or ivory. Many came to capture African people to be sold as slaves. From the early 1600s to the middle of the 1800s, about 600,000 Africans were shipped to the United States.

During the 1800s, many European countries established colonies, or countries they ruled, in Africa. They believed they were helping the Africans by introducing them to European ways. But the Africans did not want the Europeans telling them how to live. By the 1960s, most of the colonists had left or were forced out of Africa, and the former colonies became independent nations.

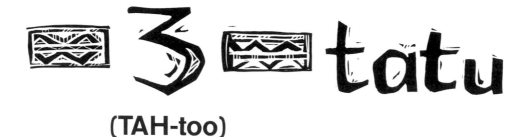 tatu

(TAH-too)

There are **three** main groups of stone structures in the ruins of the city of Great Zimbabwe: the Hill Complex, the Great Enclosure, and the Valley Complex. Most of the buildings now in ruin were built between 1200 and 1400.

The ruins have remained standing for centuries because Great Zimbabwe had skillful builders. We also know that the people knew how to make things with iron.

People in the West sometimes forget that Africans had advanced civilizations long before the Europeans arrived. The ruins at Great Zimbabwe, now part of the country of Zimbabwe, are proof of these advanced civilizations.

THE HILL COMPLEX

THE VALLEY COMPLEX

THE GREAT ENCLOSURE

4 nne

(NN-nay)

A banjo has at least **four** strings. Some banjos have as many as nine. The banjo is one of the musical instruments that were brought to the United States by African slaves.

African slaves brought much music to the United States. Jazz has African roots. So do many dances that are popular in America and in other parts of the world.

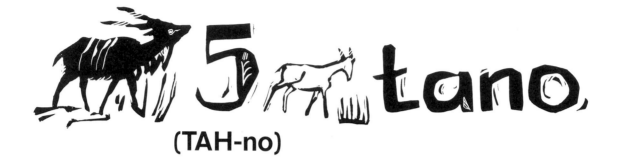

5 tano

(TAH-no)

    The Khoisan (COY-san), or Bushmen, of the Kalahari Desert rely on **five** simple tools: bow, arrow, hook, staff, and spear. With these tools, they can hunt enough food for their families.

    The Khoisan lead very hard and simple lives. They live in small groups because they can't find enough food to feed a large village. What little they have, they share with each other without question. They don't even have words in their language for hate or jealousy. Their language uses clicking sounds and is spoken very fast.

    There are not many Khoisan left in the Kalahari Desert. Progress has attracted more and more of them to the towns, where they no longer need their traditional hunting tools.

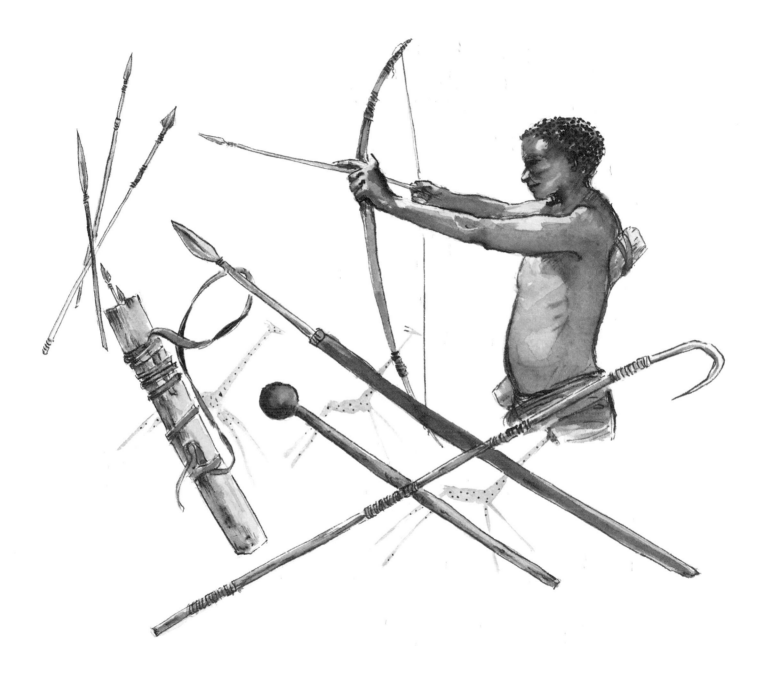

⚏ 6 ⚏ sita

(SEE-tah)

There are **six** scars on this man's face. They are the marks of his family group. They are the result of cuts made on his face during a ceremony that initiated, or admitted, him into manhood.

Initiation is very important for both boys and girls in many African families. The ceremony takes place when they are adolescents, and it celebrates their passage from childhood to adulthood. The cuts hurt, but boys and girls understand that the pain is necessary if they are to be recognized as adults.

Not all Africans have initiation ceremonies. And many Africans who live in cities no longer practice this custom. Yet some of today's African leaders proudly carry marks on their faces that they received from their tribes in adolescence.

7 saba

(SAH-bah)

Seven animals that are native to Africa are the lion, elephant, hippopotamus, ape, leopard, giraffe, and rhinoceros.

Many of these animals are in danger of becoming extinct, or dying out altogether. In some cases, the natural living places of animals have been taken over by humans for farming or for building towns. In other cases, the animals have been hunted too long by too many people. For example, the number of elephants in Africa fell from 1,300,000 to 600,000 during the 1980s. Hunters continue to kill elephants even though it is against the law.

Most African countries now have large national parks or game preserves. In them, wild animals of Africa can live and increase in number, somewhat protected from hunters and other dangers.

(NAH-nay)

Eight girls started the National Troupe of Liberia in 1965. They began traveling around Africa and the rest of the world, showing the dances, songs, and music of the different areas of Liberia.

Before the end of that year, the eight girls were joined by eight boys. By the middle of the 1980s, the National Cultural Troupe of Liberia numbered 120 dancers, musicians, and singers.

Liberia was founded in 1822 by an organization of black Americans. Some of them were freed slaves. Most of them were free blacks, people who had never been slaves. But, like the freed slaves, free blacks were not considered equal to white Americans.

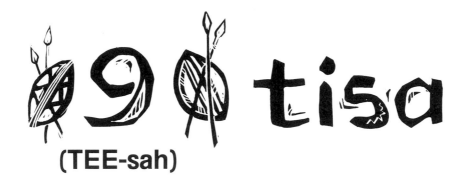

(TEE-sah)

There are **nine** lines to this poem, which is an English translation from Kinyarwanda, one of the two official languages of Rwanda (the other is French). It was sung toward the end of the 1800s by Rwanda warriors as they started out to battle. In it, they asked for the help of their king:

The heroes are called to arms.
A Mulima man invokes King Musinga.
Listen to these heroes;
They are going into battle.
Are you not also brave?
They all set out, armed with bows and spears.
You are brave in battle, we know.
The heroes will pursue those who flee.
They will attack the enemy fiercely.

Poetry and song have long been important to many African peoples. And it isn't just poets who write poems and musicians who make up songs. The warriors made up this song-poem themselves.

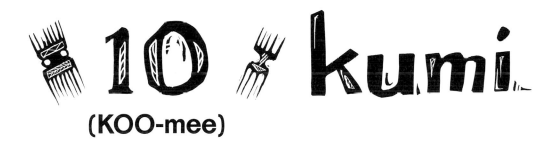

10 kumi
(KOO-mee)

There are **ten** teeth in this comb. It was made in the country of Zaire when Zaire was a colony of Belgium called the Belgian Congo. The official language of Zaire is French, but over 200 other languages are spoken there as well.

This hair comb is an everyday object. But it is also a work of art. Art in Zaire and other parts of Africa has never been something reserved for museums. African artists make beautiful objects that are useful as well.

Pronunciation Guide

1 / **moja** / MO-jah

2 / **mbili** / mm-BEE-lee

3 / **tatu** / TAH-too

4 / **nne** / NN-nay

5 / **tano** / TAH-no

6 / **sita** / SEE-tah

7 / **saba** / SAH-bah

8 / **nane** / NAH-nay

9 / **tisa** / TEE-sah

10 / **kumi** / KOO-mee